Live for, love

Patrice Lee

"Bully Me?

. . . No More!!"

By Patrice Lee

Copyright 2011

Published by Feinstein Development & Associates
Printed in the United States of America

Library of Congress Catalog-in-Publication Data

ISBN #: 9781450779609
First edition printed: July, 2011

Edited by: Mary Edwards
            Leaves of Gold Consulting, LLC
Cover Art: Bob Ivory, Jr.,
            IvoryCoast Communications
Interior Content Design: Patrice Lee

Send all correspondence to: bullyme.nomore1@gmail.com

This book is dedicated to the most wonderful and loving brother a sister could have. In loving memory of Quincey II.

Words Can Hurt, so-o-o o . . . *bad*

*"Be careful of the words you say,
Keep them soft and sweet
For you'll never know from day-to-day
Which ones you'll have to eat."*
K. McCarthy

Table of Contents

Endorsement

Life, as my family knew it, was forever changed when we experienced the deadly effects of bullying, through the loss of our beloved son Jared. He was only 13. We keep Jared's memory alive through a website that shares his story.

My family and I continue to look for answers and a way to stop the bullying. Let's rally together in this fight against bullying to protect and preserve the family's most valuable asset, our children.

"Bully Me? . . . NO MORE!!" by Patrice Lee is a rare find. In this manual, the author addresses the issue of bullying from the causes and effects of it, to offering real, practical solutions.

I recommend "Bully Me? . . . NO MORE!!" to parents and children alike for this growing problem facing our youth today. It is well worth the read.

Brenda High
Brenda High
Mother of Jared Benjamin High
www.jaredstory.com

Bully Me? . . . **NO MORE! ! !**

Preface

This book was created for children--tweens, teens-- and the parents of children who may, or may not have been bullied. It was also written for those children who may feel threatened or have become fearful of being attacked by a bully.

In it you will find questions throughout for you to respond to and assignments for the entire family. This reference manual is for your personal library.

It's time for the deadly effects of bullying to stop. The goal and the purpose of this publication is to have no more lives lost because of it.

There is a special section at the back of the book entitled, "For Bullies Only," created just for bullies, for they are looking for answers too. We address the issue of adult victims of bullying and offer supportive information for parents entitled, "Caring Moms and Dads." May this book serve you and those you care about for many years to come.

If the contents of this manual can save the life of "one child," I shall be forever grateful for that one life that was saved.

Bully Me? . . . **NO MORE! ! !**

I.

The Stats Don't Lie

Bully Me? . . . **NO MORE! ! !**

Statistics show that:

- We are losing an average of 4,400 young people per year from the effects of bullying.
- Suicide is the 3rd leading cause of death among our youth.
- Half of all suicides among children, tweens, and teens are related to bullying.
- For every suicide among our youth, there are at least 100 suicide attempts.
- Over 14% of high school students have considered it.
  - 7% of high school students have actually attempted suicide.
- According to Yale University: A bully victim is 2 – 9 times more likely to consider suicide.
  - 10 to 14 year old girls may be at an even higher risk for it.

According to ABC News:

- 30% of all students are either bullies or victims of bullying.
- 160,000 students stay home each day because of the fear of being bullied.

According to the National Institute of Occupational Safety Health (NIOSH)

- There is a loss of employment amounting to $19 billion and
- A drop in productivity of $3 billion due to workplace bullying.

University of Michigan Case Study

Researchers from the U of M Medical School looked at elementary school students from Ypsilanti, Michigan, who had exhibited conduct problems like bullying. According to Louise O'Brien, Ph.D., Assistant Professor, at University of Michigan's Sleep Disorders Center, "Children who are bullies, or have conduct problems at school, are more likely to be sleepy during the day."

It is possible that poor sleep can lead to bullying or other aggressive behaviors—a major problem that many schools are trying to address today. The researchers found that sleepiness could be caused by many factors, including chaotic home environments, fragmented sleep, or not enough sleep, because of too much electronic stimulus from televisions, cell phones or computers in the bedroom.

This study highlights that good sleep is just as essential to a healthy lifestyle as healthy eating and exercise. O'Brien said the study showed that sleepiness seemed to be the biggest driver of the behavior problems.

Michigan Chronicle, Health, June 8-14, 2011.

Note: *How's your child sleeping? If your child appears to be overly aggressive, you may want to observe their sleeping habits/conditions.*

II.

Definitions and Characteristics of a Bully

Bully Me? . . . **NO MORE! ! !**

He's Just A Bully In Disguise

There is a difference between the child who has grown up in a very loving home environment and the child who has never known or received a mother or father's love. An abused or unloved child sees the world differently, is more abrasive, and speaks a different language from the child who is loved.

It's not likely that someone will plan to become a bully. However, life's circumstances – of crushed dreams, bruised egos, and the experience of great disappointment early on - may cause that person to spiral into a state of hopeless despair, and become angry enough to hurt innocent people.

Even so, it is not o.k. to intimidate or threaten someone by saying or doing mean things to them just because you are not happy.

"Bully"

(The Dictionary Definition)

"Bully," as a noun is described as: *a noisy, blustering, overbearing fellow, more distinguished for insolence and empty* menaces, *than for courage, and disposed to provoke quarrels; as* a verb: *to insult and overbear with noise and blustering menaces; to be noisy and quarrelsome.* (American Dictionary of the English Language, Noah Webster's 1828 edition)

Related words defined: (getting a full understanding of the meaning of the word "bully")

Insolent - *to be proud and haughty, with contempt of others; domineering in power; puffed up with pride; rude; with a mean arrogance.*

Menace – *a threat or threatening; the show of a determination to inflict an evil upon another; the appearance of an evil or a probable catastrophe to come; a troublemaker.*

(Direct quote): *To show or manifest the probability of future evil or danger to; to express or show a disposition or determination to inflict punishment or other evil.*

Who Is This Bully Anyway?
(a personal definition)

A "bully" is a person--man, woman, boy or girl--with unresolved issues that cause him to have strong outbursts of anger towards others; one whose own mental anguish brings destruction to others, often affecting the mental and emotional state of being of those he attacks; one who produces such emotions as fear, anger, or despair in others; and one whose personal trauma or adversity has caused him to lash out at others in an aggressively fierce manner.

A bully is a distraction; one who keeps your mind occupied with worry and fear about his next move against you. He is on an assignment to keep you from achieving your purpose in life.

"Bullies" lash out, unexpectedly at first, for no apparent reason. They appear to be very miserable, or unhappy, and never seems to have a good day.

Many bullies have unhappy childhood memories, and could be holding a grudge against someone who caused them emotional distress months, even years ago. These people, particularly, those who never received parental love, may have experienced rejection instead. What they desire is genuine love and acceptance, but their emotions are overruled by the pain.

The absence of a parents' love during childhood may be a factor in their aggressive behavior. He/she may have been traumatized from some form of abuse; or experienced disappointment, fear, hurt, even sorrow. These unresolved issues can turn into anger.

Just as a toddler displays anger by throwing a temper tantrum, the "bully" expresses anger thru his actions against others, usually someone who appears weaker than himself. Simply put, the bully is a coward.

The Characteristics of a True Bully

You know you're in the presence of a "bully" if he is:

- very mean, or mean-spirited
- does anything to make you feel small
- has unexpected or random outbursts
- makes exaggerated statements
- embarrasses you in front of others
- makes false accusations intended for harm
- completely negative toward you most, if not all of the time
- performs often in the presence of others;
- usually loves an audience

His goal is to:

- completely deflate your self-esteem, because he has none
- crush your ego while building his own
- provoke fear in you to cover his own
- intentionally bring emotional harm to you, because he's already hurting
- shame you, for he has no conscious
- make you appear weak, and himself strong, in order to distract you or bog you down with worry about his next move

. . . and his effect(s) on the victim

- he seems larger than life itself
- it feels like it will never end
- becomes fearful
- develops poor self-esteem, has little worth
- develops feelings of helplessness, hopelessness or despair

- develops deeper levels of fear, as the bullying continues
- becomes totally engulfed, if it goes on for too long

"Bully" Classified

There are many kinds of bullies. In this book, we will highlight the ones most recognized for their offenses. Let's start with the "Classroom Bully."

The "Classroom Bully"

The classroom bully is one most of us are familiar with. The "classic" classroom bully used to be the boy who teased or picked on girls and boys in the classroom and after school. This bully has been known to taunt/tease, push, shove, take pens, pencils, and other supplies from one student and hide or put them in another student's book bag. These items were not always recovered.

Most times, the classroom bully is smart enough not to get caught and usually chooses to make his move when his classmate is most vulnerable--that is--when the teacher is out of the room. The classic classroom bully has never been gender specific.

A seat change may be the immediate solution, if the teasing begins in the classroom. The best defense is to quietly request a seat change from your teacher, as far away from him/her as possible. Hopefully, the seat change will bring total resolution to the problem.

Today, bullies are more gender specific. The boys tend to pick on boys and the girl bullies, in the classroom, tend to direct more of their attention toward other girls.

Girls and boys, young men and young women, must use caution in restrooms, hallways and back corridors of schools, buildings and unfamiliar areas. Most school hallways, bathrooms, stairwells, and cafeterias are monitored constantly for the safety of all children.

A student in middle or high school may receive more verbal bashings or physical attacks from a bully during recess or team sports, or after school. This is where boys may become more physical than they would inside of a classroom setting, particularly when the teacher is not visible.

All bullying should be reported to the proper authorities. The sooner the better. Your parents and teachers should be informed, so these conditions can be brought under control. If the bullying begins in the classroom, it may continue outside of the classroom, if not controlled right away.

The "Playground Bully"

This "bully" is probably not the best sportsman, therefore he wants to make sure no one else does well at sports. This is an area where he can really be aggressive, particularly with the boys. Girls have begun to be more aggressive with girls lately.

Sometimes he will tease and call another team member a name, other than his own. After he builds up an audience with the name calling, he proceeds to get physical by shoving or throwing balls (or other objects) toward his victim, while constantly looking for support from onlookers.

The reaction of onlookers - their support, or lack of - can play a major role here. If the other members of the team speak up, step up, or man up to the bully, it can turn this would-be bleak scenario around.

26

However, if it is not brought under control, someone can get seriously hurt. It's best for everyone to show collective support on behalf of the victim and report it to proper authorities. Being truthful may help prevent a fatality or serious injury.

"Neighborhood Bullies"

Bullies in the neighborhood are not necessarily from the local area of your residence, but could be someone who selectively chooses to zero in on your area for known or unknown reasons. This is an area where parents and good neighbors must work together through block clubs, private control cars and other methods of observance to keep their living areas safe.

"Cyber Bullies"

Growing in popularity is the "Cyber Bully." This monster bully, under the guise of social media communication, is doing some serious damage. Statistics show that girls are most often affected by it.

Peer pressure, especially boy and girl relationships, girl cliques, etc., have proven to be very detrimental. This "bully" takes all the mean things a bully would normally say in front of a small group/classroom setting and shares it in cyber space, for the whole world (World Wide Web) to see. It penetrates your spirit even more when you see it in written form, because you know that it has infinite possibilities.

Just a few negative words, on a tender topic of discussion, or one false statement, can crush ones' dreams, bruise ones' ego, deflate ones' self-esteem, and destroy ones' reputation. The devastating thing is that one does not know how long these destructive words will circulate before the dust settles. One can only imagine the continual threat of debilitating circumstances and the endless aftermath.

Children, it is important to have rules in place to monitor and control computer activity. Trust your parents/responsible adult to guide you in this area, as it will help to preserve and protect your future.

You have a purpose for being on this earth, and it wasn't to spend three or four hours a day badgering people on the internet. Your gifts can not be nurtured and developed when you are consistently unproductive.

Don't get me wrong here, Face book and Twitter have an intended purpose, and that is to enhance/improve communications worldwide. However, it was meant to be done in a positive fashion, to yield positive results and outcomes.

Cyber bullying has become one of the most deadly forms of attack, causing such devastation in children and adolescence that it has taken the lead in fatalities.

III.

Self-Assurance

Bully Me? . . . **NO MORE! ! !**

Can't You See What You've Done to Me?

Bully, can't you see what you've done to me?

I was frightened and timid.
You made me feel unsure.
It became internal; I became withdrawn.

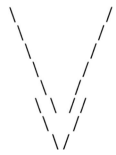

Then I decided not to let you get next to me.
I decided to (hold on and just)
Be strong! ! !

Be Strong

Let's talk for a moment about the things you do well, with little or no effort. These are your strengths. It is important that you know your strengths because during those moments when you are most vulnerable – in the presence of a bully – is when your weaknesses seem to be magnified.

What are you strengths? Name two of them. Focus on those strengths, and any new ones you discover.

It is important that you be strong, but when it comes to being bullied, you cannot do this alone. Everyone needs someone to lean on from time to time.

Children, your parents want to hear from you. Please keep the door of communication open between you so you can talk to them about anything.

Home is the best place to talk, get a hug, laugh or have a good cry. Crying relieves the body of stress. You just feel better after a good cry.

Did you know that God is never too busy, and that He never fails? He is One that you can lean on and trust at all times, no matter what.

He'll be there for you when no one else is available. You can trust Him to work on any problem or confrontation. You can draw from His strength alone.

And did you know that God says? "Vengeance is mine, I will repay." That simply means He will handle anyone who chooses to do evil, and anyone who comes against you. Your job is to pray for them and forgive their evil deeds against you.

You Need to Know **You Are a Winner ! ! !**

If you have been attacked by a "bully," first let me tell you that you are a winner. How do I know? Well, you obviously have something the bully wants. Perhaps, he sees how happy you are; or maybe you have an abundance of friends, family, and genuine people who care about your well-being. Maybe you get good grades in school and the teachers love you.

Maybe you're blessed with material things. Or, you could have just one thing he wants. Perhaps you are talented and do well on the team. Maybe you are that good looking guy or that beautiful young lady who is admired by your peers. Who knows what's on the bully's mind? He usually doesn't do a lot of reasoning with his opponents. He just attacks them out of nowhere.

Don't let the bully's behavior change you. Continue to be the great person that you are. However, you must act or react quickly, so things don't get out of hand when/or if he attacks. What I mean is, you must never allow your emotions to run wild. And never let the bully get the best of you. Even when you think he has, don't let him know it.

Trust God to handle the bully situation as only He can. For God promised us in His Word that He would fight our battles for us. He is the only One that can fight the bully and win, 'cause the bully's arms are too short to box with God. :) And that's a good thing.

Enough said about bullies. Now it's time to concentrate less on what the bully does. Instead, our focus will be on solutions to mend the brokenness it has caused, and to incorporate remedies for emotional healing from the effects of being bullied.

Spruce Yourself Up

If you've been attacked, this is the time to look your best; because the better you look, the better you will feel. And the better you feel, the more defeated the enemy - the bully - is, and will become.

That is the whole idea: to look victorious until you have the victory. **Yea!!**

Remember to let God fight this battle for you. When God is on your side, the whole world can be against you, but you still win. That's how powerful He is.

Wear your favorite clothes - styles and colors - the ones that make you feel good about yourself. Stand tall. Keep a smile on your face. Look good, feel good, be your best both inside and out, and remember: "You are the winner here!!"

In fact, it's not over until they - the onlookers, the naysayer, and of course, the bully - see that you've won.

====➜===➜

> > "Moving forward . . . " > >

Bully Me? . . . **NO MORE! ! !**

Overcoming Those Feelings of Rejection
"Sticks and stones may break my bones, but words will never hurt me." Not so.

When you've been hurt or rejected by people that you love and care about, the greatest thing that you can do is forgive them. The quicker you forgive, the faster you heal; the less chance you'll express anger, hostility, or other negative emotions.

The same rule applies to those who have been mistreated, teased or bullied by their peers. If someone has hurt, embarrassed, or humiliated you in any way, the most important thing you can do--after you report it--is forgive them. It's not as easy as it sounds, nor does it feel good at first thought; but once forgiveness is activated, the better you will feel, the healthier you will be, and the stronger you will become.

Forgiving instantly also helps you maintain a more pleasant disposition throughout the day. The goal is to have a peaceful, happy day, every day.

Another way to overcome rejection is to reverse it. In other words, look for/find humor in what the bully is saying about you and laugh at his comments. Not only will it catch him off guard, it will cause him to be confused, puzzled, dumbfounded. He will walk away defeated. Yea! You win!!

Always know that no matter what the outcome, God loves you, and He cares about all of your troubles. God's love is unconditional.

Bully Me? . . . **NO MORE! ! !**

IV.

Everything Is Gonna' Be Alright

Bully Me? . . . **NO MORE! ! !**

Change, for the Bully and Me

Hey Bully, I prayed for you today.
When I first spoke to God, I didn't know what to say.
Your words, your laughter were so fierce and strong.
"God," I said, *"This has gone on too long."*

Hey Bully, I'm prayin' for you
For what else could I do?
Your words hurt and made me (feel) sad
You made me see, God was the only true friend I
really had.

But when I prayed, do you know what I said?
"I just can't take it anymore, I'd rather be . . . ."
When I thought about the words I'd said out loud,
I asked God's forgiveness, **then, I forgave you.**

This time Bully when I pray,
I'll ask God to be a friend to you.
If you'll let Him, He'll make all things new,
'Cause you need a change in your life too.

Now, when I see you,
I look through the eyes of love.
I see a person just thirsty for real love.
I no longer see the bully that used to bother me.

Bully, God give you peace, like He gave to me.
He's the only One who can save you and set you free,
From tormenting thoughts and disturbances in your
mind, May He fill you with His love, the unconditional
kind.

You Seemed Bigger Than Life

There was a time you just seemed larger than life.
You were so full of hatred and strife.

For some reason, I just couldn't understand
How your whole day was centered around me.

I simply chose to live life happy.
And I was happy, just being me.

It was my choice not to deal with your strife.
Instead, I lifted my head in faith and believed

That God wouldn't leave me there hangin'
Because I knew He cared for me.

I simply chose to live life happy.
And I was happy, just being me.

Hey Bully!!

Hey bully,

You helped me grow
'Cause now I know
It wasn't my fault
You picked on me.

But, in the darkness
Of your glare
I could not see
Where this experience was taking me.

Now, I'm a survivor.
Can you now see, that
You were just helping me?

I had to grow
So I could help the next person
And give them a hand
So they could stand tall once again.

You Can Make It!!!

I had to grow through this
so I could help you,
just in case you became a victim too.

I just want you to know,
<u>You can make it</u>!!!!

V.

You're In the Safety Zone

Bully Me? . . . **NO MORE! ! !**

Choosing a Support System
(after you've been attacked)

Being attacked by a "bully" is draining. And, if you've been attacked more than once, you may feel overpowered, and may be looking for answers. To you I say: *"Congratulations*!! Because you survived. And if you happen to be reading this book, you're on the road to recovery."

Everyone needs help at some point in their life; and this is definitely one of those times. Please don't be ashamed or too embarrassed to ask for help.

Whether you are a child, tween, teenager, or an adult under attack, you need a support system to help you remain strong. If you already feel defeated, you need this kind of support to build you back up again.

This is where so many victims get it wrong. They wait until they are so beat up by the enemy - or bully in this case - that they have little to no strength left. Don't try to do it alone. <u>Choose a support system for yourself, immediately (upon being attacked by a bully)</u>. If you select the right support system, it will keep you strong, and stop the bully.

Some suggestions:

1. God. The Almighty One. (available 24 hrs/day)
2. Close family --mother, father, grandmother, grandfather, etc.
3. Close friends-someone you have confidence in.
4. Professional counselor – seek professional help from your pastor, school social worker, or private counselor at a local counseling agency.

5.   School principal, teacher, counselor.
6.   All of the above.

In addition to these suggestions, you might consider creating a 'bully system' or 'network' of friends who are willing to support you. This 'bully system' would make sure that you are never alone, and together you and your peers protect and support one another. There is strength in numbers.

BULLY ME? . . .

The act of one person bullying another is a battle that works on the victim emotionally and psychologically. While your interaction with a bully may not always be physical, it's one that will affect your spirit.

For the girls, the act of bullying is mostly psychological. Don't get me wrong here. This fight affects you just as much as - if not more than - a physical encounter, because everything we do or are endeavoring to become, begins in the mind.

The boys usually start working on the psyche (the mind) and move into a more physical engagement as the act of bullying progresses. The longer it progresses, the more physical it may become.

It is not recommended that you fight back, but it is imperative that you run to get help. Simply refuse to get involved physically.

You can also use God's spiritual weapons to do battle against the enemy. They are more powerful than any negative force operating through any one person.

Let God transform you through His Word. Allow Him to renew your mind and refresh your thoughts. Free yourself from being the **victim** through His Word.

For God has not given you the spirit of fear, but of power, love, and a sound mind. And, as you walk in His love, He will give you a new confidence and a new attitude towards life.

Putting Your Armor On. . .
(getting dressed for battle)

Now that we have established the fact that this battle is mostly spiritual, you need to be prepared for battle. May I present to you how to dress for the occasion?

Faithfully put your armor on just like you get dressed every day for school or work. This attire should go on before you get dressed physically. You may have already guessed that you are putting on protective gear to keep your emotions under control.

Since we have already established that this is not a flesh and blood fight, here's what you do:

1. *"Gird your loins with truth."* Purpose today to speak only words of truth.

2. *"Put on the breastplate of righteousness."* Keep a pure heart. Walk in good standing with God.

3. *"Shod your feet with the preparation of the gospel of peace."* Let peace begin and end with you. Remain calm. Everything will be alright.

4. *"Take the shield of faith to quench all the fiery darts"* that your enemy (the bully) aims at you, i.e., false accusations, unkind words or deeds, and making you the butt of his jokes. Believe only the best for yourself. Know that God loves you. *"...for it is written, Vengeance is mine; I will repay, saith the Lord"* (Romans 12:19b). And He means that.

5. *"Place the helmet of salvation upon your head."* Give your heart to Jesus. He will keep you safe. Receive Him as Lord of your life.

6. *"Take the sword of the spirit, which is the Word of God,"* and apply it to your life daily. (Taken from Ephesians 6: 10-18). There's a Bible verse for every problem and challenge you face. For all of you techie's out there, there's an app in the Bible for everything you need. Just click on it (look it up), then download God's Word into your heart. And think about it day and night.

7. *"Pray always."* Talk to God. He is real; you just can't see Him. He is available for you and desires to hear from you. He pays close attention to details. He cares that much about you. As you pray, speak God's promises from His Word and simply remind Him about them. You can have conversations with Him like this: **"God you said if I. . ."** (Recite His Words back to Him, when you find a scripture verse that you want to apply to your life.)

8. Once you've done those seven things, just stand on what you believe. Know that God is working it out for you. Now, watch it come to pass.

When you have this armor on, you surround yourself with God's presence. Once you are fully clothed, just step back and let God do the rest. :) It's that easy.

It's impossible for anyone to penetrate the presence of God around you. Now you are covered, protected, and safe; and "In His presence is fullness of joy." *This is the secret to winning the battle every time.*

Hint: Trust God. The less you complain about your problem, the sooner it will end. (Have you read about the Israelites 40 year journey in the wilderness, which should have only taken 11 days? See what happened on their journey . . . because they chose to murmur and complain.)

Your Arms are Too Short to Box with God

Bully, can't you see,
Your arms are too short to box with God and me?
I'll sit back and take it all in stride,
'Cause that's what you do with God on your side.

Bully, don't you see,
Your arms are too short to box with God and me?
Life's just a losing battle with a heavy price,
Until we realize who we are in Christ.

Now can't you see that
Your arms are too short to box with God and me?
Without Him, you'll have no rest,
No peace, no joy, nor happiness.

Oh, bully you've got to see, that
Your arms are too short to box with God and me.

I know I can do all things through Christ
Who strengthens me, even if it means
Ignoring the awful things that you do.
Hey bully, just want you to know, I'll be praying for U.

But I say unto you, *"Love your enemies, bless them that curse you, do good to them that hate you, and pray for them which despitefully use you, and persecute you"* (Matthew 5:44).

Bully Me? . . . **NO MORE! ! !**

VI.

Taking a Stand

Bully Me? . . . **NO MORE! ! !**

It's Not Your Fault, He's a Bully

It's time for the Bully to take ownership of the trouble
he's caused.
For he'll just continue if he isn't stopped.
His way of blaming you is for naught, 'cause
The bully blames the victim, when it's not the victims
fault.

You might consider prayin' for him, and try to be kind.
For he's just disturbed with emotions of a negative kind.
Doesn't mean any harm, just needs to be loved;
And to know that he's cared for by the Father above?

If the bully had known, he wouldn't have picked at YOU.

"Dodge the Ball"
"The game that continues throughout life."

Dodge ball was a game we played during gym or recess in elementary school. For me it was the most fun game of all the games we played. The idea was to dodge the ball each time it was thrown at you. You would be out of the game, if you got hit by it.

The game of dodge ball was fun, if you were the person throwing the ball, or if you successfully dodged it each time it came toward you. :) There was this great sense of accomplishment, and (a rush of honest) pride, if you were still in the game.

Now, let's transfer the idea of this game of dodge ball to your head. In doing so, your response will not be a physical reaction, but a mental one instead. Let's take a look at how we can prepare to win it without any battle scars.

In this game of dodge ball, you don't have to be good at sports. There is a real need to build your spiritual muscles. You will use inner strength and your ability to forgive, as part of your method of operation. You also will need to practice self-control.

This may require stretching your faith.

It begins with patience, positive thinking, a healthy appetite for good, integrity, and a heart filled with love. . . . It may be a little painful at first. But practicing this spiritual exercise on a regular basis will help you prepare for the balls that may come your way.

Let's look at some of the steps involved.

1. Put God first. Acknowledge God each morning and ask for His guidance and protection.
2. Keep a positive attitude and smile throughout the day.
3. Never respond in a negative way to a person who comes against you. Pretend as though you didn't hear it.
4. Forgive, even when it hurts. And let it go as soon as you forgive.
5. Report any bully activity immediately to someone in authority that you have confidence in (it must be a person who has your best interest at heart).

Now, you're ready for the ball when it comes your way. You are taking a stand each time you choose to dodge-the-ball.

Note: While you're perfecting your method of operation against enemy territory, God is fighting on your behalf.

Adult Bully's (beyond the classroom)
Adults can be bullied; and adults can be bullies too.

Since adults are reading this book too, we'll devote these next few pages on the subject to them. You may have observed or experienced the following adult behaviors.

Bullying just doesn't stop at the school or classroom level. If it isn't addressed early on, it can continue into adulthood and into the workplace as well. And sometimes, the bully just might be your boss. ☹ For lack of a better term, we will call them "Bully Bosses."

If an adult bully has authority over you, he may choose to use that authority as a weapon of mass destruction. In other words, the "bully boss," because he is the boss, might yell insulting words at you all of the time, or give you excessive workloads, as an expression of his anger.

It stands to reason that children with unresolved issues of verbal or other forms of abuse, carry or harbor those feelings of insecurity, anger, unhappiness, envy, etc., into adulthood. These negative emotions from childhood, tend to magnify in an adult as they are unmasked, causing emotional trauma to those persons who get in their way.

While bullying a child is a very serious matter, and has proven fatal, an adult bully victim may also have serious repercussions. Unfortunately, the adult person's livelihood may be affected by it, through loss of pay, demotions, etc.

If you are being bullied at work, you may be working for an unhappy or emotionally distressed manager. You may need to employ some of the same techniques you learned in elementary school (how to dodge-the-ball) as in the game of "dodge ball."

So, when you see that "bully boss" coming your way, and you know you're the target, dodge the ball. (The boss is the ball; you, are the target.) **:)** And whether you are lied on, or accused falsely, you can dodge the ball by following the steps on the previous page.

While doing those 5 steps don't forget to:

1. Watch what you're thinking and guard your thoughts carefully. Constantly refresh them with positive words and ideas.
2. Ask yourself? What can I do today to make someone else happy?

As you practice these two steps, you are building character and winning at the same time. **Winning!!** Dodge ball does have many rewards. And it feels good to win. ☺

Special note:
When you've reached the point of greatest difficulty, or are experiencing the most discomfort, is when you are closest to your victory.

Note to children: Are you surprised that bullies continue their mission into adulthood, if they aren't stopped early on? This is why you must react quickly when bullied. Seeking support does not mean you are weak, or that you're a failure. The "bully" needs to get help, and you can play a major role in him getting it.

Refuse to be Contained
(Live outside of the box)

Negative forces - the bully included - work to keep you all boxed in and in the same place year after year. The job of the enemy is to keep us where we are; to contain us. But you must resist the forces of containment.

God wants you to continue to expand and to be your best. When trouble comes your way, know that it is only a test. Don't allow past hurts and disappointments to steal your dreams.

Keep a good attitude through the difficult times, and you will see doors begin to open for you. You will experience growth, and with growth, move into a realm of endless opportunity. Here is where your dreams will begin to manifest.

So dream, and dream big.
Ask and ask big.
Expect big.
And once your receive it, dream some more.

VII.

Focus On Your Dreams

Always do your best, be your best, and expect the best.

Bully Me? . . . **NO MORE! ! !**

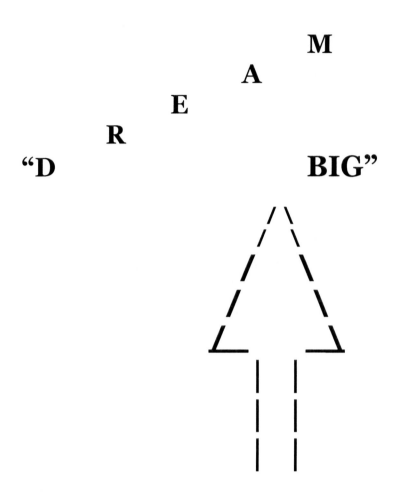

M
A
E
R
"D   BIG"

\ - - the sky is the limit - - /

Never lose sight of who you are, and where you are going.
Keep your dreams alive.

Stepping Out To Succeed
(Beyond the Attack)

Here are some things that you can do to speed up the healing process:

1. Keep a good attitude. Refresh your mind with positive thoughts and affirmations constantly.

2. Pray. Ask God for His blessings upon your life.

3. Live each day with great expectation that good things will happen for you.

4. Avoid the distractions. Don't think about past hurts and disappointments. Tune out the negative words.

5. Focus on your goals, dreams and aspirations.

6. Live each day for tomorrow, but enjoy every moment of each day.

To sum it all up:

Know that change is coming. Ask God for what you want and believe that you will receive it. Live with great expectation every day.

As you receive God's blessings, and the answers to your prayers, trust Him to work out the details. You have a wonderful future ahead of you. Set goals, write them down, plan, dream some more. The sky is the limit.

Pray

Forgive   Dream

Love

Lookin' at you through the eyes of love.

Pray.
God is always available when you call on Him. In fact He loves to hear from you. He is the only One who can change the heart of a mean-spirited person. Prayer is one of the keys to going forward.

Forgive.
Forgiveness is of utmost importance; you must forgive so that 1) you can be forgiven, 2) that your prayers can be answered, and 3) so that you can be healed emotionally. After all, God said, "Vengeance is mine. I will repay." This means He will handle anyone who chooses to do evil against you.

Dream.
When you pray, forgive. As you forgive, walk-in–love. This frees your spirit up to dream. Your mind is clear to think on good things, and your body carries no baggage from day-to-day.

Love.
This is the greatest commandment of all. Love is the driving force that propels us to forgive. "*. . . but the greatest of these is love*" (1 Corinthians 13:13b).

The body, mind and spirit are all connected. You clear your mind when you forgive. You free your spirit when you talk to God through prayer; and you feel absolutely great all over when you add the love walk to your daily regimen.

Practice looking through the eyes of love with everyone you meet. . .

VIII.

Learning to Love the Unlovable

Children (Tweens, Teens): You Are Loved

God loves you so much and His love is unconditional. He loves you even when you seem to be unlovable.

- He still loves you though you talk back, but you shouldn't speak to parents and teachers like that.
- He still loves you, even when you don't tell the truth, when you don't share with others, and when you pretend like you did your chores, but you didn't.
- He still loves you when you said you didn't eat the last cookie, but you did.
- And He still loves you though you choose not to obey. Just know there are consequences you'll have to pay.

God's love is so amazing; and it's an everlasting love. Submit yourself to Him so that you can reap all of His benefits. Once you realize the depth of His love, then you can love others through His example.

He has provided you with all of the tools needed for a successful life. You'll find these tools in the Bible. You can access them and apply them to every area of your life.

As you study His Word, you will find verses that apply to your specific area of need. If you need help, He's ready to assist you; if it's strength that you need, rely on Him for it; if you want peace, He can give it to you. The best part is that God will honor His Word if you remind Him of His promises.

Now I'm Lookin' at You . . .
Through the Eyes of Love

Everyone has a purpose for being here. God made us all unique. In His infinite wisdom, He gave us individual personalities, desires, and special gifts/talents when He made us.

The gifts that God gave you were for you to use to carry out your intended purpose for being here. Your job is to discover all of your gifts so that you can use them to bring Him honor and glory. After all, He made you. :) And He wants you to make Him proud.

Let's talk about your gifts (talents) for a moment. Many gifts are developed as children move from the toddler stage to adolescence. It is during this time that they discover music (vocal and instrumental), fine arts, crafts, wood shop and other skills. Children learn at an early age if they like music or art, science or math, communication or performing arts.

Through various hobbies, you may learn to sew, knit, crochet, make model cars, do shop metal, or develop carpentry skills. As you mature, other interests in the sciences, such as medicine, dentistry, engineering; advanced communication and all forms of technology, journalism, editing, etc. will begin to develop.

The more exposure you get - to new ideas, new knowledge, and new opportunities - the more specialized and unique you will become in your field of interest. It is understood that "gifts" developed on higher levels of learning are not pursued or achieved until one reaches a certain level of maturity (college and beyond).

I'll stop here and explain how the bully is intercepting the flow of your life as God has ordained.

Do you remember the cowardly lion from the Wizard of Oz? He was afraid of everything and everybody. He jumped, in fear, if anything around him moved. But what did he spend most of his time doing? He frightened anyone who came in his path. Not only was he a coward, he was a bully. Now do you get it?

The bully is a distraction. He is on assignment to get you off course, to make you lose sight of your purpose in this life. Once you realize that is what's happening through his actions against you, you will be able to dance all around him/her in love, like Muhammad Ali danced around his opponents, before he finally gave them the finishing punch.

Now, you're not going to punch the bully, or knock him out, but by ignoring his tactics and walking-in-Christ-like-love, he will become defeated. He will see that you are not affected by his antics any longer, and it will be quite obvious to those looking on that you are winning at this game of dodge ball. :) Did I say **winning?** Yes, you are a winner!!! **YEA!!**

So, smile at him/her, and when you smile, it will make him lose his focus on you. SMILE!!!!! **:)** And keep smiling. **:)**

Your assignment **#1**: Rent or buy the *Wizard of Oz* DVD and study the lions' behavioral patterns carefully. You'll have one up on the bully the next time you see him coming your way.

You Made Me Realize

You made me realize how special I was.
There was something I had
   . . . something you wanted
   . . . something you needed
   . . . something you found in me.

There was something

In your life you were lacking
   . . . you were looking
   . . . you were searching for.
   . . . You just needed
    "LOVE."

Dear God,

I thank you for parents who have always loved me.
I pray that you'd bless that bully to find in You
The **"love"** he (she) so desperately needs.

Bully Me? . . . **NO MORE! ! !**

=====➔=====➔

> > **"I'm moving forward"** > >

Bully Me? . . . **NO MORE! ! !**

Moving Forward =➜ ===➜ ===➜
===➜ ===➜ ===➜ ===➜ ===➜

No one likes the clothes you wear? *Develop your own style. Maybe you'll be the next household name in the fashion industry.*

They won't accept you in their circle of friends? *It doesn't matter. You need real friends. Learn to be more selective. Your time is too valuable to waste on people that don't want anything out of life. It helps to surround yourself with people who are smarter than you.*

Is someone talkin' about you on Face book? *Now this one's a little tough. How do you ignore that? Well, you simply rise above it . . . them.*

Whenever you are ridiculed or criticized overtly, the opinions expressed usually don't have as much significance to you as the 'why' behind it. Case in point: It's not so much what people do to us that causes us detriment, it's the motive behind their action that we continue to think about.

If someone speaks unfavorably about you, whether you hear them say it or not, it affects you on the inside. If you don't address it immediately, it may cause emotional damage. Address it right away.

It penetrates your spirit even more when you see it in written form, even worse, if what they've said isn't true. That pain is magnified if the bully has posted something on face book or twitter.

Now it's visible for the entire cyber space world to see. Use it to your advantage. When you respond, let it be an open communication of forgiveness for the world to see. What a shining example you will be.

Your response to the cyber world might be as follows:

"The steps I take today (each day) are directly linked to my future. That is why I must remain focused on achieving my goals. Perhaps then, God will use my humility to help me achieve extraordinary things. Therefore, I selectively choose to forgive you for the actions you've taken against me." (Your name)

By raising the bar for yourself, and keeping your standards high, you can rise above the chatter and tune out the noise. Know that God's desire for you is a life filled with blessings and favor, when you put your trust in Him.

Always be willing to forgive the person who has hurt, embarrassed or humiliated you in any way. Forgiveness is of vital importance for a pain-free recovery. Know that God will back you up, if you ask Him to do so. And He is always concerned about what troubles you.

"Casting all your care upon Him; for He careth for you" (1 Peter 5:7).

". . . Vengeance is mine; I will repay, saith the Lord" (Romans 12:19b).

IX.

Making Wise Decisions

You Are God's Creation . . .
And you are wonderfully made

Think about it. What a wonderful creation it was when God made you! There is no one exactly like you. There is only one you. That means you are unique, exceptional, rare, and that's good. :)

You will need a pen and paper for this section. Now, let's get started.

What special characteristics/features make you unique? Hint: If you can't think of a special characteristic. I'll think of one for you, "Your fingerprints."

List three things about yourself that you love. What talents/gifts do you have? What is it that you do well? What are the 'little things' that make you happy?

What 'little thing' can you do for someone else today to bring them joy? Hint: Why not start with your family, i.e., Mom, Dad, grandmother/father?

When you think about others, and send a little kindness their way, you will have less time to worry about your own problems.

Your assignment #2: Answer all of the questions on this page. Share the answers with your Mom and Dad.

"I will praise thee; for I am fearfully and wonderfully made" (Psalm 139:14a).

You Are Here For a Reason

It is important for you to know that God created you on purpose. Therefore you were born with a purpose and for that purpose to be carried out. You are so special that no one can do it for you. In fact, you are irreplaceable.

You might be the next great scientist, inventor, or product developer; for there are some discoveries yet to be revealed, some innovations yet to be created, and puzzles that need to be solved. There are products that have yet to be developed and cures that need to be found.

Are you willing to let God do great things through you? The world is waiting for your contribution.

Now that you understand that you have a purpose for being here, you must find out what your purpose is. If you are not sure what it is, ask God: "What was I created to do?" Or you might ask: "What is my purpose for being here?"

Once you know the purpose for which you were born, humbly submit yourself to God's plan for your life. Let nothing/no one keep you from achieving your God-given purpose.

"For I know the plans I have for you, declares the Lord, plans to prosper you and not to harm you, plans to give you hope and a future" (Jeremiah 29:11, niv).

Your Decision

God hears you each time you pray, but He is a personal God and loving Father. His desire is to have a personal relationship with you and a "heart-to-heart" talk every day.

If you have never received His Son, Jesus as your Lord and Savior, a good time - the best time - the right time is now. Let Him make your life brand new.

Say this out loud:

"Today I ask to be forgiven for sins known and unknown. Heavenly Father, I believe you sent your only begotten Son, Jesus Christ, to die for my sins, that He was buried and arose on the third day. I believe His shed blood cleanses me from all unrighteousness, and now I am made righteous before You Father because of His blood. I accept You as my personal Lord and Savior, and right now I am born again."

You will get to know God better if you'll take some time to read His Word. The more time spent reading the Bible, the less complicated your life will be. The answers to all of your problems are found there.

Now, you can wake up happy. Give yourself the first smile of each day. And think on good things.

Expect God's favor to go before you, and plan to be a blessing everywhere you go. Expect to receive His blessings along the way.

Train Your Thoughts?

As a man thinketh in His heart, so is he. In other words, we are what we think. What we think is what we say. What we talk about and dwell on is what we ultimately become.

Become aware of your thoughts. Take control of them, before they take control of you. Be consciously aware of what you are thinking at all times.

Set your mind on things above, not on the things of this earth. This means you are not to be concerned with the cares of this world.

God has equipped you with the ability to do whatever you put your mind to do. He can strengthen you to do what might ordinarily seem impossible to do.

God will take away fear as you develop your faith. The more time you spend reading His Word, the greater your faith will be. The greater your faith, the stronger you will become. You will find that faith in God cancels all fear, doubt, and disbelief.

Happiness is a decision. You decide to be happy, or not. When you wake up happy, a smile will come easy for you.

Talk Back

As you begin to grow stronger, you will see your faith increase. Now you will be able to speak to your situation and cause the mountain of adversity to crumble as you speak to it.

Here's something you can say:

"I choose to forgive those who have come against me, both past and present. I will not harbor ill thoughts and I will hold no grudge(s) against them. I will be strong and of good courage, as I am standing on the Word of God." Know that you can have whatever you say. So begin to speak the words that you desire to have.

For example, you might say:

"I know that I am a winner, and I have not been given the spirit of fear, but of power, of love and a sound mind. I am the head, not the tail, above only, not beneath. I speak to the mountain of adversity to move out of my way, so that I can accomplish what I have been called/destined to do. I will successfully achieve my purpose on earth, and nothing shall stand in my way. I am excited about life. I am excited about this day and what I will accomplish. Father, I choose to honor You in all that I say and do. I thank You God for healing me from every form of bondage, deception, all lies, false accusations, hurt, disappointment, all verbal and physical abuse, anguish, betrayal and shame. Thank You Lord for setting me free."

Conquering the Bully

You can conquer the bully if you:
- Ignore him/her (if possible)
- Keep your distance
- Replace fear with faith
- Travel in multiples, not alone
- Seek wise counsel
- (Children) Talk to your parents/ responsible adult
- (Parents) Listen to your children

Key points to remember: **Survival Tidbits**

• Know that you are somebody special. Your life has special meaning to your family members and closest friends, because there is only one you. Be selective with whom and what you give your time, attention and talents to.

• Stay away from troublemakers and naysayers. Don't pay attention to the cruel comments they make. Keep looking up. Keep moving forward.

• If you have been attacked by a bully, it's not recommended that you fight back, but it is imperative that you report it immediately. You are not just getting support for yourself. You could be very instrumental in helping the bully get the attention he/she needs too.

• Keep your parents/responsible adult(s) informed about each incident every time you are attacked. Talk it out. Forgive that person(s). And keep talking to your parents/family/loved ones until you feel better.

• Replace the pain (of being embarrassed or humiliated) with positive thoughts, activities and kind deeds. Try to take your mind off of yourself, i.e., you might look for other children who have been bullied like yourself and reach out to them by offering your support.

• If you were bullied on the way to school, consider carpooling, or take a different route. Try to surround yourself, when possible, with people who have your best interest at heart.

• Don't allow distractions to keep you from achieving your purpose in life. Live each day for your future, because your future is bright.

• To avoid distractions, keep your thoughts elevated above the chatter (frivolous conversations).

• Remember always to look your best, be your best, do your best. Keep a positive attitude at all times.

• Smile from the inside out. One smile can make a difference in your outcome.

• Learn to dodge the ball and have fun doing it. Play the game of dodge ball and win.

• The true champion is one who knows how to ignore the enemy. Don't try to win every battle yourself. Let God do the fighting for you. Use the spiritual weapons He gave you.

• Let peace begin with you. Be kind to yourself and others.

Your assignment **#3**: Study the characteristics of the mighty eagle. You can look it up on the internet or check out a book from the library for this one.

X.

Caring Moms and Dads

Bully Me? . . . **NO MORE! ! !**

Bully Me? . . . **NO MORE! ! !**

Caring Moms and Dads:

This Section Is For You   =======
```
                              |
                              |
                              |
                              |
                              |
                        \\  |  //
                         \\|//
                          \| /
```

Children are our most precious asset of the family
constitution.

Bully Me? . . . **NO MORE! ! !**

Using Your God-Given Authority
Cyberspace: Attacking the activity.

Mom and Dad, it's time to get back to the basics. Good communication is vital to establishing and maintaining a healthy home environment for your family.

As parents, you will experience many rewards if you lay the foundation, and work at keeping an open dialogue for conversations between you and your children. It is important that they feel comfortable discussing their problems with you.

You are the authority in your home, and you will have to take control of the computer activity in your home, even if it means removing key parts of the PC, restricting hours on the internet, shutting it down for a duration, cell phone usage restrictions, etc.

It's up to you to exercise your God-given authority at all times. It's also important that you control the length of cyber time usage and monitor the cyber activity in your home.

After you have established some ground rules, encourage your children to use the internet wisely, i.e., for educational purposes. Show them how this and other family-engaged activities on the computer can work to their advantage. Let social media time be a family activity too.

You can use the internet as a source to extract valuable information, and find creative ways to make it a fun experience. (Don't forget about the games you can play on it.)

The computer can also be used to do research and to attain knowledge. Far too many students complete college, only to realize they've chosen the wrong career for themselves, after receiving their degree. Why not help your children get a jumpstart on their career(s) before they go to college?

Through research . . . many careers have flourished . . . . . many discoveries have been made . . . many cures have been found, and through research . . . you can improve your life and the lives of others.

Assignment **#4:** Why not start today? Have your children research topics related to their interests. Let learning together be a rewarding experience.

"Seest thou a man diligent in his business? he shall stand before kings; he shall not stand before mean men" (Proverbs 22:29).

Looking For Answers
(in all the right places)

The Word of God says that we are to train up a child in the way he should go, and when that child is old, he will not depart from it. To train up a child God's way, is to live, by example, and teach your child/children how to use the Bible as a standard for daily living.

In so doing, you live the life He desires for you to have, a life full of faith, filled with the blessings and the favor of God; subduing evil. There is nothing more powerful than the spoken Word.

Parents, if you are not teaching your children the Word of God, start today. There is protection, safety, comfort, healing, life, wisdom, peace, joy, power, love, refuge and strength in the Word of God.

Your children need all of this to stand against the bully and other forces of evil. If you set the example, they will follow your lead.

Your assignment: Be sure you arm your children with the Word of God. It works like a sword against evil-doers.

Note: You may want to have your children write the verses from the Bible on 3 x 5 cards. This will make it easier for them to memorize these life-changing Words of God. Please note the Bible verses on pg. 94.

A Parents' Guide:

Dear Moms and Dads,

Children who are taught of the Lord have great peace. In this section of the book, I will share some verses from the Bible that will bring life, healing and increase to you and your children.

First, let your children know how important their words are by sharing the following with them: Your words—the words that you speak—will either work for you or against you.

Teach your child to speak words of life, because *"Death and life are in the power of the tongue: and they that love it shall eat the fruit thereof"* (Proverbs 18:21). The words we say should speak life to us. Choose your words wisely.

These verses from the Bible will build faith and increase endurance for any trouble that may come your child's way. As these Words of Life are applied to their lives, they will come to know and enjoy the peace of God that surpasses all understanding.

"The Lord is on my side; I will not fear: what can man do unto me?" (Psalm 118:6).

"No weapon formed against me shall prosper..." (Isaiah 54:17a).

"If God be for us (me), who can be against us (me)?" (Roman8:31b).

"We are (I am) more than conquerors through Him who loved us (me)" (Romans 8:37).

"I can do all things through Christ which strengtheneth me" (Philippians 4:13).

Taking Authority Through Prayer

Loving Parents,

We cannot be with our children to protect them every moment of the day. It is possible, however, to "bully-proof" your children through prayer and Word confessions each day. The prayer on the following page, if incorporated into your child's life daily, will yield positive life-changing results.

The living words they will say will increase their faith in a loving God and develop their confidence in His Word. It will cause them to be victorious in every area of life.

This prayer is so positively good; the whole family can use it too. You and your children will know that you can do anything you put your hands to, with God's help, as He has promised to strengthen you along the way.

Parent Note: If you have not received Jesus as Lord and Savior of your life, I extend an invitation to you today. The salvation prayer is found on page 82.

Bully-Proof Your Child in Prayer
(with Living Words)

Let your child know that God is omniscient, omnipotent, and omnipresent. God knows all things, is all-powerful, and is everywhere at all times.

Have your child say the following prayer, at the start of each day, to activate God's protection and favor upon his/her life.

_____'s **Prayer:**
(Your child's name goes here)

"Good Morning God. Today will be a great day, if You will travel with me. Thank you for the angels you have placed all around me that protect me and keep me safe from harm.

I believe that Your Word, which I speak, will do what you say it will do.

I am so thankful that you will take care of anyone who comes against me, for you said vengeance belongs to You. That means I will never have to fight back. I believe your promise which says, You will cause even my enemies to be at peace with me.

I know You will never leave me, nor will You ever forsake me. Thank You God that whenever I need You, You will always be there for me.

I will stay in your presence all day, because in your presence is so much joy. Thank you for keeping me in perfect peace.

God, I love You. Thank you for caring so much about me. This is my prayer to You in Jesus' name. Amen."

Bully-Proof Your Child with Words of Life

Use the following confession to increase your child's faith in a loving God, to build a protective wall around his heart and emotions, and give him the confident assurance of God's presence at all times. Let him know that because God is present, and lives in his heart, there is no need for him to fear.

_____'s **Confession**: (Say it everyday)
(Your child's name)

"God says that I am fearfully and wonderfully made. I am the head, and not the tail. I am above only, and not beneath. And I am first, and not last."

I believe God's Word which says that, "No weapon formed against me shall prosper, nor will it cause me any harm. God is my refuge and strength, a very present help in trouble.

I choose to think on good things, do kind deeds, and share good information. I will make a positive difference in those whose lives I touch. I want to impact the world with good.

Today I will find things to laugh about and keep a happy heart, because laughter is like a medicine (for me). It keeps me well."

Bully Me? . . . **NO MORE! ! !**

XI.

For **Bullies** Only

Bully Me? . . . **NO MORE! ! !**

This Section is

For Bullies Only:

You may have been wondering what this book is about, so the following segment was created just for you.

Bully Me? . . . **NO MORE! ! !**

Who's Controlling You?

Everyone has adversity or has suffered some kind of affliction. Everyone has experienced disappointment or had some sadness in their life. And it's the enemy's job to keep you discouraged during the tough times. If you're experiencing adversity, climb that mountain one step at a time and trust God.

Do you know who the enemy is? There is but one enemy - satan - who manipulates the minds of people to do evil things. For the enemy comes to steal, kill, and to destroy.

The comedian, Flip Wilson, made this concept quite easy to understand. Some of you parents may remember Flip Wilson. Each time he stepped into a special character and did something he shouldn't have, he'd smile sheepishly and say, "The devil made me do it."

He was absolutely right; for God will never tell you to do anything wrong. God is good and does only that which is good. He loves you too much to invoke/ bring evil on you in any way.

"The thief cometh not, but for to steal, and to kill, and to destroy: I am come that they might have life, and that they might have it more abundantly" (John 10:10).

You Must Decide:

Are You a Chicken, Crab or an Eagle?

Hey Bully,

It's time for you to decide. You've spent a lot of time making other people miserable and you probably don't even know why. Well, I'd like to give you something to think about. Here's my story about the chickens, crabs and eagles.

First, it is important to know who each animal is as it relates to human characteristics and the relative comparisons. Please read about them and make a decision about your future.

In this <u>example</u>:
"Chickens" – represent the general public usually the people with no clear direction

"Crabs" – are the people that try to hold you back from achieving anything

"Eagles" – are our leaders, movers and shakers; our great servicemen and women; those who know how and enjoy serving others with unconditional love; an ordinary person who does extraordinary things; one who uses all the talents and gifts God has given him/her; etc.

Life is full of chickens, crabs, and eagles. Which one are you?

Now let me explain how they work in their little circles of influence:

Chickens peck around back and forth, with no clear sense of direction, never straying far from the chicken coop? Crabs on the other hand are stored in a barrel. Once in, each crab makes sure the other crab never gets out.

The eagle - who is described as rare, strong, unique, powerful - is driven to excel. Eagles are known and admired for their strength. Eagles fly high. Eagles fly so high that crows, who like to pester him constantly, are unable to reach him.

Wouldn't you rather be an eagle? In order to be an eagle, you must change the direction of your travels and chart a new course. You must rise above the coop mentality and get out of the barrel.

You, my friend, can change directions by changing your attitude. By adjusting your attitude you can lift the altitude of your mind and elevate your thoughts.

As you learn to love yourself, then you will be able to love your neighbor. As you begin to see the world through the eyes of love, your life will take on new meaning. Things will become fresh and new, and the old will pass away.

Know that you can soar like the eagle . . . because you are somebody special.

Your assignment: Study the habits/characteristics of the mighty eagle.

After Thoughts
(The act of bullying creates a thin line between life and death).

The bullies didn't realize their actions would help lead to a fatality. In a special interview presented on MSNBC's *Today Show,* the bully had many regrets for the actions he'd taken against the bully victim who committed suicide.

But, it was too late for the bully victim, who had endured more than three (3) months of name calling, degrading words in cyberspace, and threats of physical attack. It was just too much.

And now it's too late for those charged with criminal behavior/assault; for the damage is already done. But it doesn't have to be that way for you.

Do you really want to throw your life, your reputation, and a promising future away? Is being a bully worth your being convicted and maybe doing jail time, or perhaps being imprisoned for life?

Don't wait until it's too late. Stop the bullying now. You can turn your life around today. The decision is up to you.

Your Decision
(from the your heart to God's)

God hears you each time you pray, but He is a personal God and a loving Father. His desire is to have a personal relationship with you and a "heart-to-heart" talk with you every day.

If you have never received Jesus, as your personal Lord and Savior, a good time - the best time - the right time is now. You need Him in your life today. Let Him make your life brand new.

<u>Say this out loud</u>: "Heavenly Father, I come to you in the name of Jesus. Please forgive me for being so mean to others. Forgive me for being a bully and for hurting so many innocent people. I believe you can heal me from every form of abuse, hurt, heartache, pain, disappointment, rejection, and the fear of being rejected again. I want to clean up my life and change how I think. I am ready to exchange the way I've been living, for the better life that you have for me."

<u>Now pray this out loud</u>:

"Lord, I believe that you sent your only begotten Son, Jesus Christ, to die on the cross for my sins, and that He was buried in the grave and arose on the third day. I believe His shed blood cleanses me from all unrighteousness, and now I am made righteous before the Father. I accept you as my personal Lord and Savior, and right now I am born again."

Congratulations! This is a very special day for you. Keep a record of this day and celebrate your day of new beginnings each year. We celebrate the most important decision of your life.

It's Not That Complicated

God's Word can change your thoughts, words and actions.

Your mind is always busy with thoughts. Some thoughts are good and some are not. You will say and eventually become what you continue to think about, and your mind has a lot to do with it.

There's a natural pull of man to do evil, because of the sinful nature of the first man, Adam. Consequently, you must take advantage of every opportunity to fill your mind with good thoughts, positive affirmations, and the wonderful promises of God to avoid it.

How we think, how we feel, and what we say is controlled by the activity of the brain, the mind. Whether you are having a great day or a not so wonderful day, the mind has something to do with it.

If you are constantly thinking jealous thoughts, you will express those feelings of envy through your actions. If you are angry, you will express anger; and an angry man or woman is never at a peaceful state. If you are upset or at a state of unrest, you will upset others around you, and will cause a state of unrest wherever you go.

The good thing is that you can, on purpose, change the way you are thinking to improve the quality of your life. You can make a conscious effort to live a more productive life by spending time in God's Word.

Life will become less complicated when you refresh your mind daily with His wonderful Words of Life.

Bully Me? . . . NO MORE! ! !

XII.

Care Enough to Share

Bully Me? . . . **NO MORE! ! !**

Showing That You Care:

If you can save the life of one child by sharing this book, would you do it?

Too many lives have already been lost, because parents and children were not informed.   Let's become proactive about bully prevention. Let's work together to preserve our future generations.

Maybe you know a child, or children (tween or teenager) that could benefit from the information provided in this manual. By sharing this information you will help preserve the sanctity of life.

If you picked up this book out of curiosity, we encourage you to share it. Buy an extra copy for someone else's child or consider giving this book away, just because you care.

Recommended reading: "How to Overcome Every Obstacle . . . and Land on Top" by Patrice Lee.

http://behavioral-management.com/bullying-statistics
(March 28, 2011)

Kids Who Bully Are Twice As Likely To Have Sleep Problems, Study Finds. Michigan Chronicle, Health, June 8-14, 2011

God's Word: *The Bible*

Bully Me? . . . Review Questions

1. Most bullies are unhappy.   T/F

2. The bully's attack is merely an expression of past hurt, anger, or disappointment.   T/F

3. Name three places you can go to get support if you have been bullied.

4. If you become a bully victim, what is the first thing you should do?

5. Name seven non-violent ways you can arm yourself against bully attacks.

6. List three characteristics about yourself that make you wonderfully unique. (It's o.k. to brag about you here.) :)

7. What is the greatest spiritual gift of expression you can put into action? (Hint: Love never fails.)

8. What are the four things you can do to help you look through eyes of love?

9. Name four types of bullies.

10. What can you do to support someone who may have been bullied?

11. How can showing support for others help you?

12. Can you explain the game of dodge ball if you are confronted by a classroom bully or a bully boss?

13. How can the internet be used as a tool to enhance your future?

14. To let peace begin with you is a good habit to practice.   T/F

15. What can you do at school/in your neighborhood to stop the bullying now? Know that you can make a difference.

16. Remember: The bully's arms are too short to box with God. :)

NO MORE! ! !

Bully Me? . . . **NO MORE! ! !**

To order additional books of 10 or more, go to:
www.bullyme-nomore.net

Patrice Lee continues to write and publish books. She is available to speak to corporations, church youth groups, at conferences, seminars, to middle and high schools students, and parent organizations.

If this book has helped you in any way, please share it with us. We would be happy to receive your comments at: bullyme.nomore1@gmail.com